Native American Lives

Carrie Cavender Schommer

Dakota Language Teacher

Written by Diane Wilson

Illustrated by Cole Redhorse Taylor

Minnesota Humanities Center

Lerner Publications ◆ Minneapolis

GENEROUSLY SUPPORTED BY

This book has been supported by the Minnesota Humanities Center, generously funded through the Shakopee Mdewakanton Sioux Community (SMSC) through its Understand Native Minnesota campaign, also funded in part by the Arts and Cultural Heritage Fund that was created with the vote of the people of Minnesota on November 4, 2008, and the National Endowment for the Humanities.

Lerner Publications Company
An imprint of Lerner Publishing Group, Inc.
241 First Avenue North
Minneapolis, MN 55401 USA

For reading levels and more information, look up this title at www.lernerbooks.com.

Illustration credits: Cole Redhorse Taylor
Additional image credits: family photos courtesy of Carrie Cavender Schommer, back cover, pp. 6, 32, 38; courtesy of Upper Sioux Community, by Angela Ochoa, p. 12; Seth Eastman/Minneapolis Institute of Art, p. 14; Laura Westlund p. 15; public domain, p. 19; Office of Governor Tim Walz & Lt. Governor Peggy Flanagan, p. 42. Background pattern: Anastasiia Gevko/Shutterstock.

Main body text set in Noto Serif. Typeface provided by Google Open Source.

Library of Congress Cataloging-in-Publication Data

Names: Wilson, Diane, 1954– author. | Taylor, Cole Redhorse, illustrator.
Title: Carrie Cavender Schommer : Dakota language teacher / written by Diane Wilson ; illustrated by Cole Redhorse Taylor.
Description: Minneapolis : Lerner Publications, 2026. | Series: Native American lives | Includes bibliographical references and index. | Audience: Ages 9–14 | Audience: Grades 4–6 | Summary: "Carrie Cavender Schommer spent decades teaching Dakota language and culture at the University of Minnesota and in her home community. From growing up to life as an educator, explore the inspiring life of Schommer"– Provided by publisher.
Identifiers: LCCN 2024049791 (print) | LCCN 2024049792 (ebook) | ISBN 9798765671818 (paperback) | ISBN 9798765680018 (epub)
Subjects: LCSH: Schommer, Carrie Cavender, 1930––Juvenile literature. | Dakota teachers–Minnesota–Biography–Juvenile literature. | Dakota Indians–Minnesota–Biography–Juvenile literature. | Dakota Indians–History–Juvenile literature. | LCGFT: Biographies.
Classification: LCC PM1021 .W55 2026 (print) | LCC PM1021 (ebook) | DDC 497/.5243092 [B]–dc23/eng/20250213

LC record available at https://lccn.loc.gov/2024049791
LC ebook record available at https://lccn.loc.gov/2024049792

Manufactured in the United States of America
1-1012018-54283-3/3/2025

Table of Contents

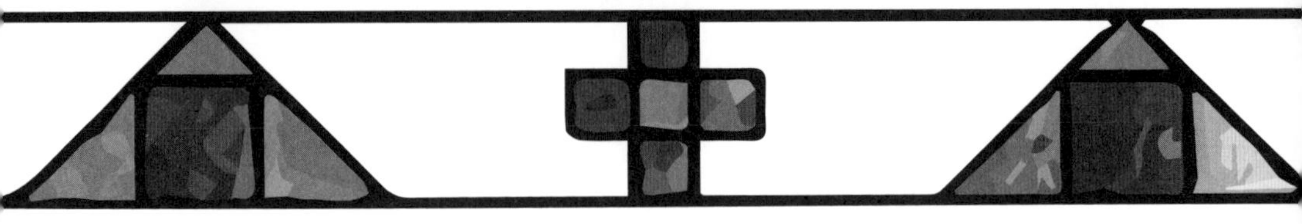

Introduction

Storytelling, a traditional tool of many Indigenous peoples, is alive and well among Native Americans of many nations. The authors, illustrators, and editors of this series, who are all Dakota or Ojibwe, continue their cultural traditions in creating these books and telling stories of leaders, athletes, teachers, and artists.

This series of books is by, for, and about Dakota and Anishinaabe (Ojibwe) and other Indigenous peoples. In portraying our histories, knowledge ways, culture keepers, and beloved figures, these biographies help Dakota, Anishinaabe, and other Native American children imagine their own potential for full futures.

We prefer to be called by our tribal names (Dakota, Ojibwe, or Anishinabe) or "Native American" or "Indigenous." We use "Indian" in numerous

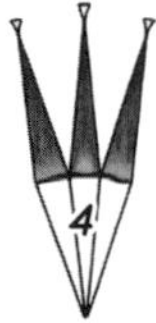

contexts today, such as the “National Museum of the American Indian.” In this series, you will see the use of the term “Indian” in historical context, and not as a derogatory name.

We hope readers will consider how the facts of social barriers based on race, culture, education, and class are part of the life stories in these books. History, especially the impacts of treaties, underlies these stories as well. The legacy of forced education in the English language by government and religious schools, poverty, and the disruption of family life are also themes. The Indigenous peoples featured in these narratives overcame such circumstances. Natural talent in art and sports, leadership skills, and Native American cultural strengths are also themes of their stories.

This series includes stories of historical figures who lived, worked, and broke barriers a hundred years ago, as well as the ongoing accomplishments of exceptional Ojibwe and Dakota people who became leaders, athletes, teachers, and artists, and whose life stories are meaningful today. Our hope is that you see yourselves in the extraordinary lives presented in these books.

—Gwen N. Westerman and Heid E. Erdrich,
series editors, May 2024

Carrie Cavender Schommer

Wahpetoŋwiŋ

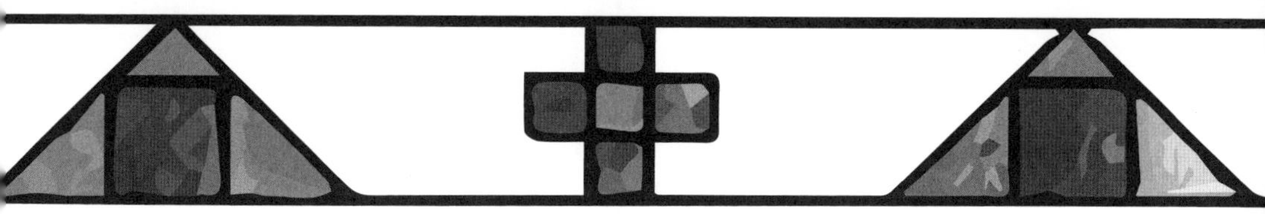

Chapter 1
A Love for Languages

On Carolynn Cavender's first day of school in 1935, she walked to the bus stop with her father, William Cavender. She could feel her heart racing with nervous excitement as she waited with her brothers and a close friend. Carrie had never ridden a school bus before. Her family only spoke the Dakota language at home. She didn't even know how to tell the teacher in English if she needed to go to the bathroom.

"Carrie," her friend said, calling her by her nickname. "Don't worry. You'll be fine." With those encouraging words, Carrie climbed the steps of the bus.

Carrie's teachers were kind and patient in helping her learn to speak English. She enjoyed meeting new people and making friends. Every day she discovered new things to tell her parents about, like the fountain that brought water with a turn of a knob. At home, Carrie's family drank fresh water from a pail. Sometimes the school lunch made her stomach feel sick. And she didn't like resting on a rug in the afternoon.

Every day after school, Carrie's father met her at the bus stop. As they walked down the long gravel road to their home near the Minnesota River, he asked Carrie what she learned that day. Even when Carrie was tired, she always liked to talk! Sometimes her father helped her understand new words she had heard that day.

As a young girl, Carrie showed a gift for learning languages. She spoke Dakota with her family and friends. Her mother, Eliza Roberts, only knew a few words of English. If Roberts wanted Carrie to pick carrots in their garden, she would tell her in Dakota, "Paŋgi zizi uŋge ok'a," which means "dig carrots." But Roberts also wanted Carrie to practice English every day at school and at home. Carrie learned quickly and earned good grades in all her classes.

Carrie began to understand why her parents thought it was important to learn this second language and culture. The world was changing quickly for Dakota people, and their language was changing with it. Carrie and her siblings were among the last generation in her community to grow up speaking Dakota as their first language. As fewer people spoke Dakota, her family and friends used English more and more.

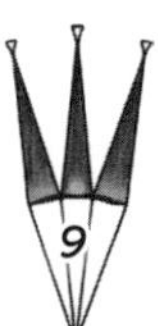

Map of Dakota Dialects

The Santee, or Eastern Dakota, live near the lakes and woods along the Minnesota River and Red River, and speak the Dakota dialect. The Yankton Dakota live on the prairies and speak both Dakota and Nakota dialects. The Teton, or Western Dakota, live on the plains and speak the Lakota dialect. These groups make up the Oceti Ṡakowiŋ (oh-cheh-tee shah-koh-ween).

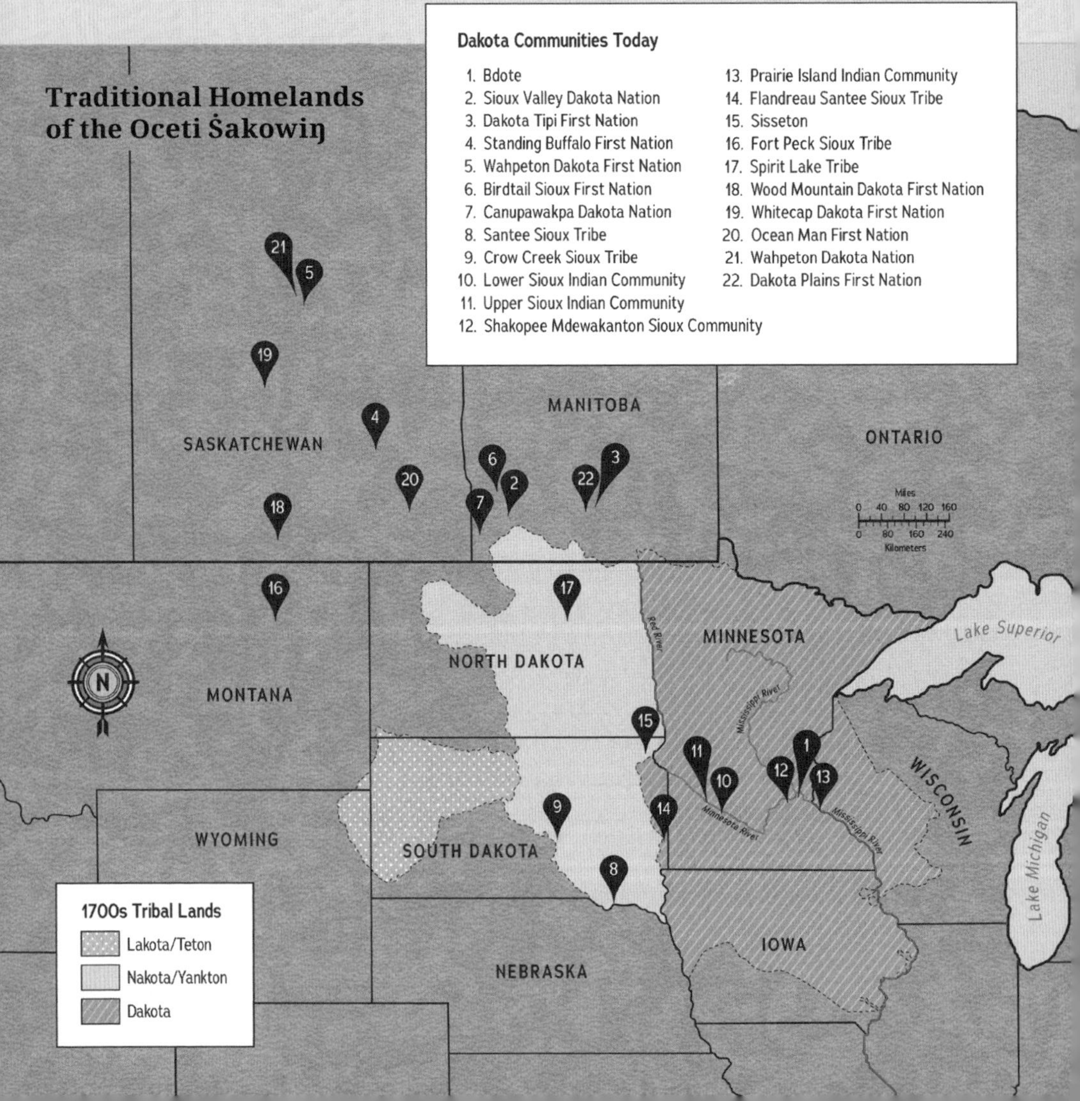

As an adult, Schommer would use her gift for learning to become a Dakota language teacher. Over her long career, she taught thousands of students about Dakota language and culture. Her life and work have inspired many people to learn Dakota so that the language will continue to be spoken.

Chapter 2

A Dakota Way of Life

The story of Carrie's family began long ago. Carrie grew up hearing stories about her grandparents and great-grandparents, as well as her other ancestors. Knowing Dakota history helps people understand why the language and culture have changed over time, and why it was so important for Carrie to become a teacher.

For many generations, Carrie's family has belonged to the Wahpeton band of Dakota, also known as "people who dwell in the forest." The Wahpeton people have lived in what is now Minnesota for more than a thousand years. Carrie's family lives with their community near the Minnesota River at Pezihutazizi Kapi Makoce,

The Dakota People

French fur traders and explorers learned about the Dakota from neighboring Indigenous tribes who called them "Nadouessioux." As more and more Europeans came into the region, they called the Dakota "Sioux." For Dakota people, "Dakota" means "friendly" or "ally."

which means "the place where they dig for yellow medicine." This area is also known as the Upper Sioux Indian Community.

The Dakota people are part of the Oceti Sakowiŋ, or Seven Council Fires. These seven bands live in different areas across parts of Canada, Nebraska, North and South Dakota, Montana, and Minnesota. They speak three different versions of the Dakota language. The Santee, or Eastern Dakota, speak the Dakota dialect. They live near the lakes and woods along the Minnesota River and Red River. The Yankton, or Central

Dakota, speak Dakota and Nakota and live on the prairies. The Teton, or Western Dakota, who live on the plains in South Dakota, speak Lakota.

A hundred years before Carrie was born, many Dakota families lived in a large territory in the southern half of Minnesota. They had no electricity or stores to buy food, so they had to be smart about feeding their families. Throughout the year, they moved between camps to gather enough food to live through each winter. They knew where to hunt and fish and where to find plants they used as medicine. They knew which foods were ready in each season. Dakota people always thanked the plants and animals for giving their lives as food. This way of living was healthy for people and for the land.

In the summer, Dakota families built bark lodges that stayed cool in hot weather. The men and boys fished and hunted for small game. The women and girls gathered early spring fruits such as wild strawberries. They planted corn, beans, and squash. These plants are sometimes called the Three Sisters because they help one another grow. In late August, they used birch bark canoes to harvest wild rice on shallow lakes. The women dried their surplus food and stored it underground for the winter.

Dacotah Village (1849–1855) by artist Seth Eastman

Whether hunting or harvesting, Dakota families were careful to take only what they needed. They left food for other people and for the animals. They took care of one another so no one was hungry. Dakota people believe everyone and everything is a relative to be treated with respect.

After ricing season, the men went deer hunting and the women dried the meat so they would have enough for the winter. When the snow came, they moved to their winter camps where families lived in warm tipis made from bison or deer hides. Winter was a good time for telling stories around the fire. Many years later, Carrie would share these same stories with her own children.

During this time, Dakota people did not need books or a written language. Oral stories repeated many times helped them remember their history. A good storyteller knew how to entertain by making stories come alive. Each year, stories called winter counts were told about important events so they would not be forgotten. Old stories called ohuŋkaŋkaŋ were about spirit beings, such as the trickster Uŋktomi. Grandparents also told stories to help children learn how to behave.

After a long winter, people were excited to move to their maple sugar camps. As the snow began to melt, they tapped trees to make maple syrup and sugar. This was a welcome treat! Their leaders watched the

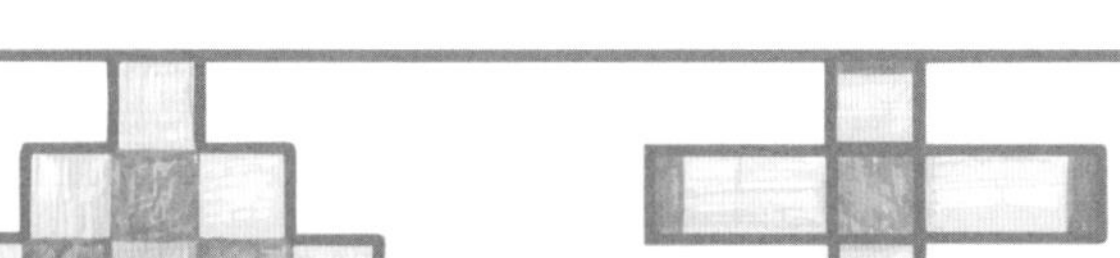

stars so they would know when it was time to move to the summer camps.

Carrie's ancestors lived this way for many years. They passed these traditions on to the next generation so children such as Carrie would grow up knowing how to live as Dakota people.

But in the 1800s, this way of life began to change as the US government pressured the Dakota people to sell their land.

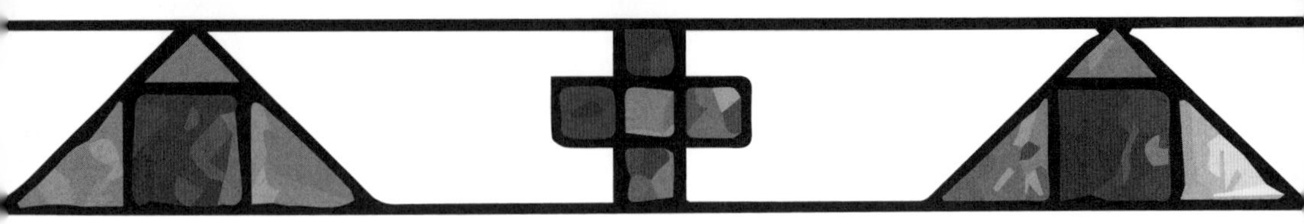

Chapter 3

Treaties Claim Dakota Land

One of the family stories Carrie learned as a child was about her great-grandfather, Mazamani, Iron Walker. He was born in 1820 and grew up to become a chief of the Wahpeton people. Carrie's auntie and grandparents used to tell her stories about his courage and strength as a leader. Hearing these stories helped Carrie understand how important it was to help her people.

Mazamani grew up spending summers with his family at Iŋyaŋ Ceyaka Otoŋwe, a village on the Minnesota River that would later be called Little Rapids. During his lifetime, Mazamani

Mazamani, Iron Walker

would see many changes as explorers, traders, settlers, and immigrants brought new ideas, goods, and tools. When he was a young man, the United States government began asking Dakota people to sell their land in exchange for food and payments.

Government agents wanted the Dakota people to change how they lived and to speak English. They wanted Dakota men to learn to farm and own land. But the men wanted to keep hunting as they always had, while the women cared for the gardens.

Some churches sent missionaries to teach Dakota people to become Christians. They did not understand that Dakota men and women were already spiritual people with different beliefs they had followed for years.

In 1843, missionary Stephen R. Riggs visited their community. Mazamani had become a respected chief who took care of his people. On this visit, Riggs hoped to set up a mission or church in the village to preach about Christianity. Mazamani turned him away.

Several years later, in 1852, Carrie's grandmother was born. Maza Okiye Wiŋ, Woman Who Talks to Iron, was the daughter of Mazamani and his wife, Haza Wiŋ, Blueberry Woman. Like Carrie, she grew up surrounded by her tioṡpaye, or extended family, which included aunts, uncles, cousins, and grandparents. Everyone helped care for children and teach them kinship terms—a polite way of speaking to each family member instead of calling them by their name.

The tioṡpaye also helped young boys and girls learn important life skills. Everyone had a role in helping care for their community. While they learned different skills, boys and girls were equally important. Maza Okiye Wiŋ learned from her mother and aunts how to garden and care for the home. She used a sharp tool called an awl to punch holes in pieces of leather before stitching

them together with deer sinew to make moccasins and bags. Even as a young girl, she was known for her excellent quillwork and beadwork. She knew how to clean hides, make clothing, and dry the food they grew and gathered. These skills helped Maza Okiye Wiŋ learn how to care for the family she would have in the future.

While Maza Okiye Wiŋ was still a young child, the US military forced her community to leave their land and change their seasonal way of life. Maza Okiye Wiŋ was among the last generation of children who spent their summers at Iŋyaŋ Ceyaka Otoŋwe. More than one hundred years later, Carrie would visit this lost village with an archaeologist to see where her family had lived.

Shortly after Minnesota became a state in 1858, Mazamani traveled to Washington, DC, to help negotiate a new treaty. The government wanted the Dakotas to sell half of their reservation land in the Minnesota River Valley. Mazamani did his best to protect his people and keep peace with settlers. Despite his efforts, the Dakota people were now on the brink of a devastating war.

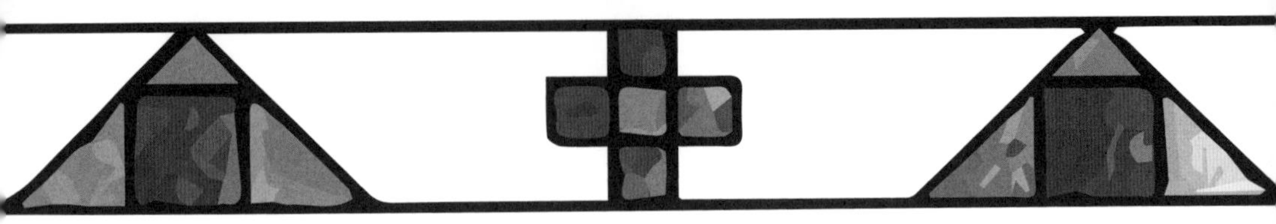

Chapter 4

The US-Dakota War of 1862

By 1862, Mazamani was hearing from Dakota people that they were frustrated with this new way of life. They were angry about the government's broken promises. Under pressure to change who they were, the Dakota did not feel respected. The government agent kept their food locked in a warehouse so families could not feed their hungry children. The treaty payment was late, and traders would not give them credit to buy food. One trader, Andrew Myrick, said that if people were hungry, "let them eat grass."

On a warm August night, the tension erupted in a

war between some of the Dakota and settlers. Other Dakota tried to protect settlers from harm. After six weeks of fighting, the Dakota were defeated. In hasty and unfair trials, 303 warriors were found guilty. About seventeen hundred women, children, and elders were forced to march to a concentration camp at Fort Snelling for the winter. Thirty-eight warriors were hanged at Mankato. This was the largest mass hanging in the country.

Governor Alexander Ramsey said that all Dakota had to be removed from the state. In the spring of 1863, they were shipped by boat to the Crow Creek Reservation in South Dakota. The government broke their treaties with the Dakota and seized their land. The Dakota were no longer allowed to live on their homeland.

Maza Okiye Wiŋ and her great-grandmother, Haza Wiŋ, were among the Dakota who were sent to the Crow Creek Reservation. Hundreds of Dakota adults and children died from hunger and sickness. Many of the warriors were sent to a prison camp near Davenport, Iowa. Some families escaped to Canada and other areas farther west. This was a sad and lonely time for Dakota people as their families and communities were broken apart. Carrie learned that their prayers helped them survive.

Carrie's Ancestors

The story of Maza Okiye Wiŋ and her experience during the war has been passed down in Schommer's family. Maza Okiye Wiŋ watched her father, Mazamani, try to make peace. He carried the white flag of truce as he walked into the soldiers' camp. He was wounded instead and was carried to a nearby village where he died. Maza Okiye Wiŋ was only ten years old. Her father was buried on a ridge of land that would one day be returned to the Dakota people.

Like many Native Americans, Carrie's family had a history impacted by non-Native education. Beginning in 1879, the government funded hundreds of boarding and religious schools around the country. Native children were required to attend and were sometimes taken from their families. At school, they were not allowed to speak their language or pray in their own way. The schools wanted Dakota children to speak English and act like American people. Over the next one hundred years, use of Dakota language would slowly decline. The loss of Dakota language speakers would one day inspire Carrie to become a teacher.

In the 1880s, some Dakota people returned to Minnesota and settled in the Upper Sioux area. Maza

Okiye Wiŋ came home with her husband, Iyaŋgmaŋi Hoksida, Running Walker Boy. He was the son of Wahpeton Chief Iyaŋgmani. Carrie's grandparents had become Christians with new names, Isabel and John Roberts. Despite the changes they had lived through, they were still Dakota. They became leaders in their community who worked to help their people, just as Mazamani had done.

Isabel and John Roberts raised their family to speak the Dakota language and know their culture. By passing their knowledge to their children, they kept their culture strong for a new generation. One of their daughters, Eliza Roberts, would become Carrie's mother.

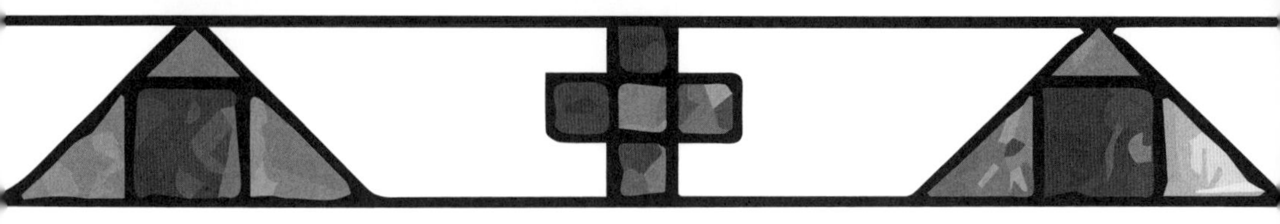

Chapter 5
Growing Up Dakota

On the cold winter day of March 12, 1930, Carolynn Isabel Cavender was born at home in a village called Hekute, right below the bluffs. Her grandfather John Roberts saw her black hair and said she was a real Dakota baby. He named her Wahpetoŋwiŋ, Leaf Dweller Woman. Her middle name came from her grandmother Isabel.

Carrie and her ten siblings grew up in a busy, lively family where they all learned the Dakota language. Their grandparents and other relatives lived nearby, close enough to visit often. Tall cottonwood trees grew along the nearby banks of the Minnesota River, where they liked to fish and swim. Large, white pelicans flew overhead each spring

as they migrated north. Carrie's father planted a big garden every summer, growing vegetables and traditional corn.

As a young girl, Carrie liked to be outdoors as much as possible, exploring and picking berries in the summertime. Some days, she and her cousins filled an empty syrup pail with sandwiches and hiked to Firefly Creek to eat lunch. Afterward, they lay in the grass and watched the clouds make different shapes. In winter, they went sledding or built a snowman.

Since their house did not have electricity, Carrie's father bought a radio that he hooked up to car batteries. On New Year's Eve, they lay on the floor and listened to the parties going on in big cities. They had a Victrola record player that had to be wound with a crank handle to listen to music on vinyl records.

Carrie's father, William Cavender, walked miles into Granite Falls each day for his job as a butcher. He had attended a government school growing up that taught Native children to speak English and become Christians. Cavender learned Dakota as a child from his family, so he grew up bilingual—speaking two languages.

Not all Dakota children went to government or religious schools. Carrie's mother, Eliza Roberts,

attended a country school and only spoke Dakota. She knew the traditional Dakota ways of caring for her family. She cooked meals with vegetables from their garden, meat they hunted, or fish they caught from the river. She knew which plants to gather as medicine when they were sick.

By growing up close to the land and her family, Carrie learned about plants and animals, as well as caring for her community.

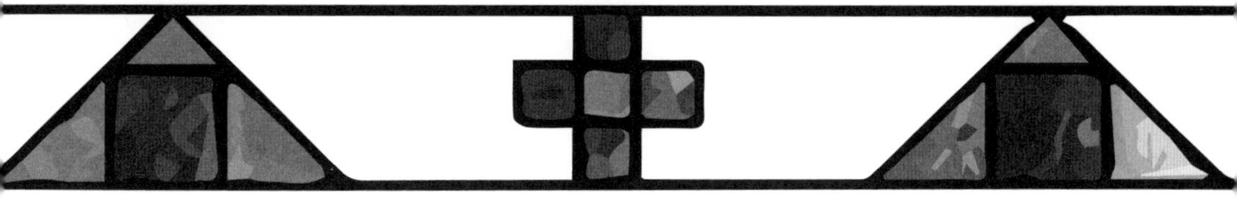

Chapter 6

Living in a Changing World

When Carrie turned five, her parents decided that she would go to the new school in Granite Falls to learn to speak wasicu, their word for the English language. Looking back as an adult, Carrie would say, “They were the most difficult steps I ever took in my whole life because I knew that that was going to change our world.”

At first, Carrie’s father told her to speak English only at school. Her mother disagreed and said, “No, they have to bring it home in order for them to retain that language.” Her mother knew her children would need to speak English in order to survive in the world.

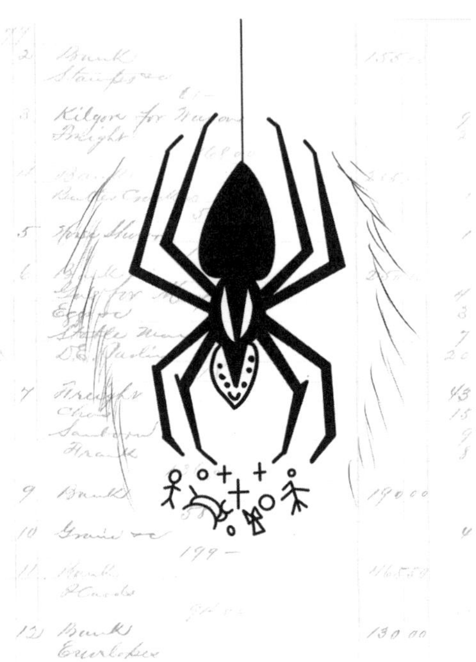

At home, Carrie learned Dakota history and culture from the oral stories that were shared by her grandparents and aunties and uncles. Elders told stories so their history would always be remembered. Knowing they were true stories made them even more exciting. Auntie Annie told stories about Uŋktomi—a character who sometimes gets into trouble but teaches us important lessons—that made Carrie feel as though she was living in the story. Her grandfather John Roberts told them about the war in 1862 that forced their Dakota relatives to leave their homeland.

These stories told a different history from the books Carrie read in school. Those books did not include oral stories that came from Dakota elders' lives. Instead, Carrie learned about history the way that non-Native people understood it.

When Carrie was about to start ninth grade, she

asked her father if she could go to the Flandreau Indian School in South Dakota. Only a few Dakota students attended the school in Granite Falls. She wanted to see more Native people and learn about their cultures and languages. He told her, “You can try it. If you don’t like it, don’t try to run away or anything.”

Carrie went to Flandreau, but she was disappointed to find she didn’t learn more about different tribes. Instead, it was a government school that only taught US history and culture that did not include a Native perspective.

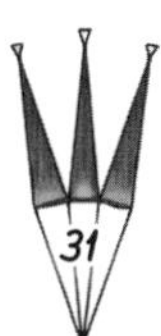

Carrie Schommer

"I used to hear some of the young men from out West out in the campus singing their traditional songs," Carrie said. "They were never asked to sing at assemblies. . . . That was heartbreaking. I felt so bad for them because of how lonely it must be for them to think of home way over there."

Carrie made good friends at Flandreau but decided to go home to Granite Falls after tenth grade. By the time she graduated from high school, she had learned to live in a world that was very different from the way her grandmother Maza Okiye Wiŋ had grown up. Carrie was bilingual and knew how to succeed in public schools. Her parents had raised her as a strong Dakota woman who would always remember her language, history, and culture.

As a young adult, it was time for Carrie to figure out how she could use her gifts to help her people.

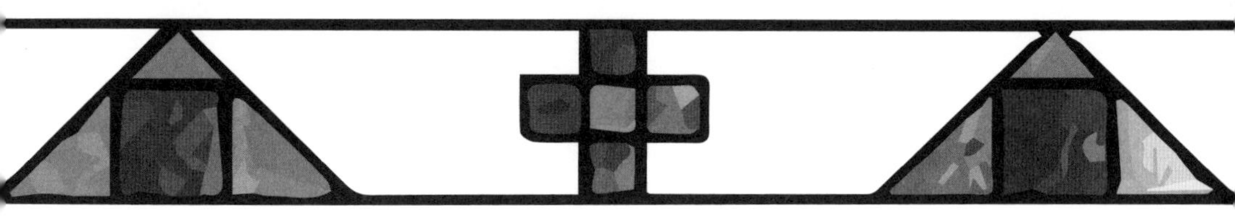

Chapter 7

Teaching the Dakota Language

After graduating from high school in 1948, Carrie left home to study at Hamline University in St. Paul, Minnesota. She attended for a year before leaving to marry Edward Schommer, who was Catholic. They raised their six children to be Dakota and Catholic. Carrie's parents lived with them during the winter and shared stories with their grandchildren. As a family, they attended many cultural events in the Twin Cities.

While Schommer raised her children, new programs around the country helped Native people learn their languages and cultures. At the University

of Minnesota in Minneapolis, Roger Buffalohead and others created the first Department of American Indian Studies in 1969. They wanted to offer Dakota and Ojibwe language classes for students. They knew that many of their students did not learn their language at home. One of the best ways to help students understand their Dakota or Ojibwe identity is to teach them to speak their language.

After Schommer went to a feast hosted by the Department of American Indian Studies, they asked if she would help teach the Dakota language. They believed she would be a good teacher because Dakota was the first language she learned as a child. In 1976, after taking a course to become accredited as a teacher, Schommer started teaching Dakota with two elders.

For the next twenty-three years, Schommer taught Dakota language and culture to university students. She helped develop a curriculum, the teacher's plan for what students need to learn each day. Bringing cultural programs to the students and the community was an essential part of her work. Sometimes, Schommer and the elders in her department had to stand their ground and insist on protecting the culture and working with their communities.

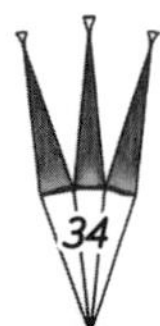

Writing the Dakota Language

Missionaries and brothers Gideon and Samuel Pond developed the first written Dakota language in the 1830s. As they learned the Dakota language, they created a written alphabet and a dictionary. They wanted to translate the Bible into Dakota so they could teach people to become Christians. The Dakota stories they translated were often changed to show their own beliefs.

"One thing we always did—and you need always to do that—at the beginning of each quarter we would always have a feast," Schommer said, referring to a gathering of Native people to celebrate an occasion with a big meal. "You have to do that to bring that part of the culture in to strengthen the students and ourselves. But all during the school year, we always made ourselves available to the communities out there so they would understand and know what we were doing."

In addition to teaching many students, the Dakota language teachers also developed a better system for writing the language. Schommer believed that turning the oral Dakota language into written English

words without losing the meaning was a difficult challenge for anyone. “The total language structure is much different from the English,” Schommer said. “No literal translation can be made from either language into the other.”

Working with other teachers and a linguist, Schommer helped develop an orthography, or writing system, that was closer to the oral language. This allowed students to learn how to pronounce words using the Dakota alphabet. Schommer also worked with her department to publish the language book *Dakota Iapi* for students in 1978.

In 1999, the elders that Schommer had been teaching alongside for many years chose to retire. After they were gone, she walked across campus to teach her first day of class. Suddenly, the loss of the elders made her feel sad and lonely. She thought to herself, “I am the only one left.” She sat down on a bench and prayed about what she should do next. She realized that she didn’t want to teach at the university any longer. Schommer decided to retire at the end of the year.

But that didn’t stop her from teaching Dakota language and culture in other ways. Schommer knew how important it was for young people to learn.

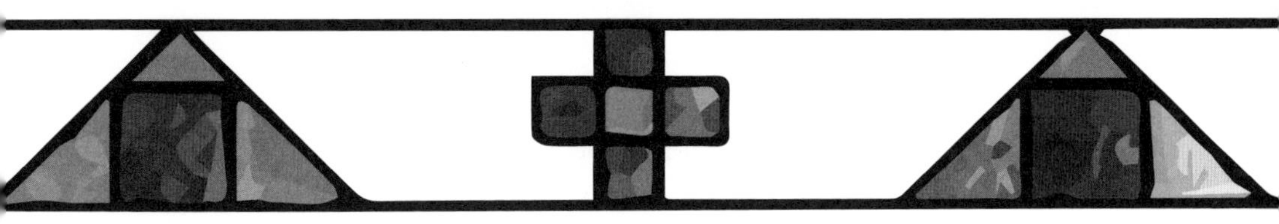

Chapter 8

Coming Home as a Teacher

After leaving the University of Minnesota, Schommer taught Dakota language and culture classes for four years at the Shakopee Mdewakanton Sioux Community. She was well known throughout the state and beyond for her work helping to revitalize the Dakota language. Students often called her Kunsi Carrie, or Grandmother Carrie, a kinship term that showed respect and affection.

In 2003, Schommer began teaching at the same Granite Falls school where she first learned to speak English. Some of her students lacked any understanding of their Dakota identity. Schommer

began by explaining about the Oceti Sakowin, Seven Council Fires. Then she asked them to go home and ask their parents which band they were from. "You need to first start from your home base, your family," Schommer said.

Schommer and her students

Even though her students were just beginning to learn the Dakota language, Kunsi Carrie did not teach Dakota as their second language. She told her students, who grew up speaking English, that Dakota is their first language.

"The reason why I want to do things in that way is because I want them to feel within them who they are," Schommer explained. "That is who they are. Not the wasicu that they've been doing all these years. Their inner self is what's very important." Without the strength that comes from knowing who they are, young people can get caught up in making bad choices. "I want them to know themselves and

who they are and always be proud of yourself," she added.

As a teacher, Schommer knew that children learned best if they were taught in a positive, patient manner, the same way she was taught as a child. She believed that Native students are equal to everyone in the classroom, including the teacher. Sometimes the students can even be the teachers to the teacher.

For example, while Schommer knows how to use computers, she didn't know about new technology, such as iPads. But because iPads were important to her students, she worked with them to figure out a new Dakota word for it.

Schommer has dedicated her life and career to helping young people know their Dakota identity. Her daughter, Dawn Schommer Chase, said that her mother "loves working with youth. That's her passion. She's always praying for the young people. They're always in her heart."

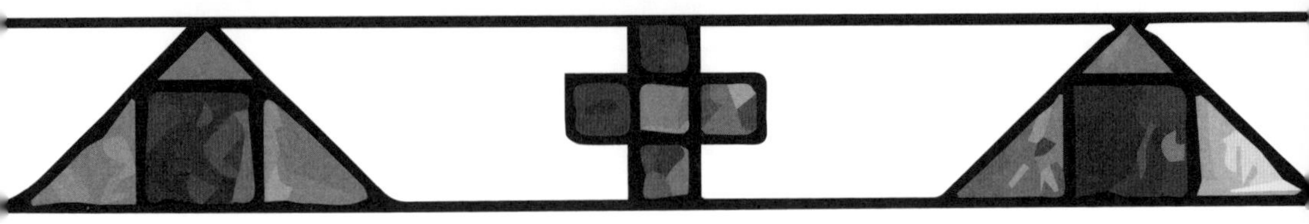

Chapter 9

Sharing Language and Stories

Schommer has helped many other people with their language and history projects. She wrote the foreword for the 1992 reprinting of missionary Stephen R. Riggs's dictionary, first published in 1852. In the foreword, Schommer wrote, "The Dakota language and culture are one and the same. The language is the foundation of the Dakota culture."

In the mid-1980s, Schommer met anthropologist Janet Spector, who was researching Dakota life at Iŋyaŋ Ceyaka Otoŋwe. They visited the site together, and Schommer shared stories about her grandmother Maza Okiye Wiŋ. Spector included the

story of Schommer's family in her 1993 book *What This Awl Means: Feminist Archaeology at a Wahpeton Dakota Village.*

Schommer also worked with her granddaughter, Waziyatawin, to translate the stories of Dakota elder Eli Taylor. His stories in the 2005 book *Remember This! Dakota Decolonization and the Eli Taylor Narratives* were published in Dakota and English. Waziyatawin is a Dakota scholar working to protect Dakota language and culture.

In 2002, a group of Dakota language speakers founded Dakota Wicohaŋ to teach Dakota language and culture to families. In 2013, they released the documentary *Dakota Iapi Teunhindapi,* which included interviews with Schommer and other elders. She explained in the companion booklet that reclaiming our language comes through kinship and family.

Schommer was also active in supporting positive change for her family and community. Many years after Chief Mazamani was buried high on a ridge, the Minnesota government turned that land into a state park that included his grave. Schommer's family and community had to pay a fee to visit his grave and their own homeland. This felt wrong to them. For

Schommer (*third from right*) attends a ceremony on March 15, 2024, when Minnesota Governor Tim Walz (*second from right*) and Lieutenant Governor Peggy Flanagan (*third from left*) sign legislation to return land to the Upper Sioux Community.

many years, they asked that this land be returned to the tribe. Finally, on March 15, 2024, Governor Tim Walz signed legislation returning this land to the Upper Sioux Community. Schommer and her family attended the signing ceremony.

"Grandfather, grandmother, father and mother made this path for us that we walk on," Schommer said. Her words remind us that learning the language is one of the ways that Dakota people are reclaiming their culture and traditions.

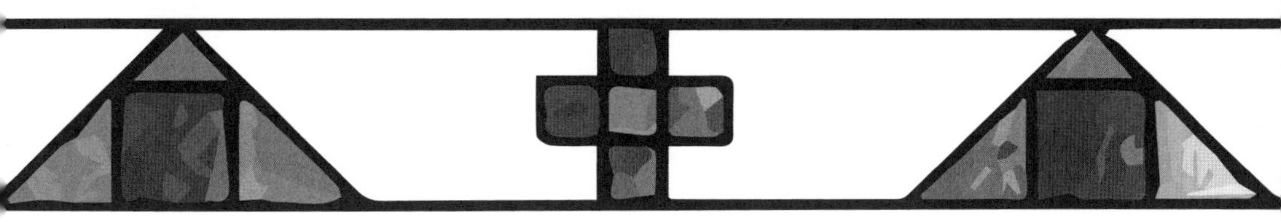

Chapter 10

Reclaiming the Dakota Language

In 2024, ninety-four-year-old Schommer was old enough to remember her grandparents' stories of the 1862 Dakota War. She was also one of the oldest-remaining first language Dakota speakers in Minnesota. Although she is retired from teaching, Schommer still loves to tell stories and explain Dakota words. Her generous nature, combined with a long career of teaching, have made her a well-loved regional treasure.

Schommer's contribution to language revitalization was recognized in 2016 with a Lifetime Achievement Award that was presented at the Minnesota Indian

Schommer at the Minnesota Indian Education banquet in 2016

Education banquet. She spoke with humility about receiving this great honor. "It was more like receiving an award for a part of your life that was given to you by Creator," she said. "In the Native way, that means living your whole life as who you were meant to be."

For Schommer, that meant remembering many valuable lessons that she learned from her elders about Dakota culture. "We're supposed to have respect for life, whether it be red, white, or black," she said. These lessons also help Schommer stay optimistic. As the number of Dakota language speakers has declined drastically, people sometimes say that the language is lost. But Schommer disagrees. She believes that if students learn Dakota well, the language will go on in the next generations.

When asked what she would wish for Dakota people, Kunsi Carrie replied, “I would like to see bringing back the language for the children to share as they’re growing up. And you can’t take just the language alone; you need to take the culture and the language, you can’t separate them, they’re both the same . . . the culture and the language are one.”

Through her work, Schommer has carried on the legacy of a Yankton anthropologist and linguist Ella Cara Deloria. When Schommer was a child, Deloria worked in South Dakota to preserve the Dakota language and stories.

Kunsi Carrie has been a good relative to Dakota people throughout her life. She taught thousands of students to speak the Dakota language. Her work helped many people from all backgrounds understand who Dakota people are. Schommer’s love for young people helped them heal by learning their language and identity. Her devotion to her community will help preserve the Dakota language and culture.

At a recent language meeting, she said, “Close your eyes, and we are all the same.”

Historical Context

The Dakota and Ojibwe people have histories as rich and full of struggle as the US or other countries. This timeline presents important events in one place as a reminder that no one human history is more important than another, but history often makes it look that way. This timeline also provides context from the Dakota and Ojibwe histories. You can use it to respond to the book by comparing the timelines of each person featured in this series to the events listed here.

Beyond memory, this place called Mni Sota Makoce, or Minnesota, is where the people became Dakota. They traveled as far north as Hudson Bay in Canada, as far west as the Rocky Mountains, south to trade with the Pueblo, and to the southeast past the trading city of Cahokia to the southeastern part of what became the United States.

During this same time, Anishinaabeg, the larger group that includes Ojibwe people, lived far to the east of Minnesota, near the Atlantic Ocean. A series of prophecies, or visions of their future, set the Ojibwe off on their five-hundred-year journey to find a new home in “a land where food grows on water,” (meaning manoomin, wild rice) along the Great Lakes and eventually in Minnesota.

Timeline

900–1400	The Dakota live, as they have always, in what will become Minnesota; ancestors of other Indigenous groups, including the Ojibwe, begin migrating west.
1540–1622	Spanish and French explorers map the Mississippi River and Dakota village sites and make contact with the Ojibwe at Lake Superior.
1730–1850	Ojibwe and Dakota fight over Dakota territories; battles end with their peace agreement in 1870, which remains unbroken.
1776–1783	The American Revolution is fought.
1805	The Dakota agree to sell land to the US government, but the US government never pays.
1819	Fort St. Anthony, renamed Fort Snelling in 1825, is built at Bdote (meeting place of rivers in present-day St. Paul, Minnesota).
1825	The Dakota and Ojibwe lose land in the Prairie du Chien treaty.
1830	Congress passes the Indian Removal Act, forcing all Native Americans to move west of the Mississippi River.
1837–1850s	Treaties force the Dakota and Ojibwe onto reservations, and they lose hundreds of millions of acres of homeland.
1849–1857	Minnesota Territory is established, and American settlers encroach on Dakota lands.

1858	Minnesota becomes a state.
1861–1865	The American Civil War is fought.
1862	War between the Dakota and the US begins in August and ends in September.
1863	The US repeals treaties, and almost all Dakota are removed from Minnesota.
1880s	The Dakota people begin to return to their communities in Minnesota.
1924	Congress passes the Indian Citizenship Act, granting citizenship to all Native Americans.
1930	**Carolynn (Carrie) Cavender is born.**
1935	**Carrie begins attending Flandreau Indian School at the age of five.**
1948	**She starts college at Hamline University in St. Paul, Minnesota.**
1953	The US makes laws to end the legal status of tribes as nations during the years known as the Termination era.
1956	The Indian Relocation Act passes to move Native Americans off reservations to cities.
1976	**Schommer begins teaching the Dakota language.**

1978 The American Indian Religious Freedom Act ends the outlaw of a tribe's religious and cultural practices. **Schommer helps publish the student language book *Dakota lapi*.**

2005 **Schommer's Dakota translations are published in *Remember This! Dakota Decolonization and the Eli Taylor Narratives*.**

2016 **Schommer receives the Lifetime Achievement Award at the Minnesota Indian Education banquet.**

2024 **Schommer witnesses Governor Walz presenting legislation returning land to the Upper Sioux Community.**

Glossary

anthropologist: a person who carries out research in the field of anthropology, the study of human beings or human nature

dialect: a form or variety of a language of a specific region in respect to vocabulary, pronunciation, and other ways of speech

immigrant: a person who comes to settle permanently in another country or region, as viewed from the perspective of those already living in that land

kinship: ties of relationship by birth, marriage, or ritual that form the basis of social organization

linguist: a person who is skilled in the learning or use of languages; a person who specializes in the structure or historical development of one or more languages; an interpreter or translator

missionary: a person sent on a religious mission to convert people to Christianity

oral: relating to communication by speech; relating to a tradition, culture, society, etc., in which the spoken word is the chief form of communication and shared from generation to generation

reservation: an area of land held and governed by a Native American tribal nation

Source Notes

22 Kenneth Carley, *The Dakota War of 1862* (St. Paul, MN: Minnesota Historical Society, 1976), 6.

29 "There Were About Five of Us That Started School in Granite Falls with Not a Word of English," Minnesota Historical Society, December 4, 2024, https://www.usdakotawar.org/stories/contributors/carrie-schommer/1113.

29 Diane Wilson, “Carrolynn (Carrie) Schommer,” Phillips Indian Educators, accessed February 21, 2025. https://www.pieducators.com/wisdom/carrie_schommer.

31 “There Were About Five of Us.”

32 Wilson, “Carrolynn.”

35 Wilson.

36 Gwen Westerman and Bruce White, *Mni Sota Makoce: The Land of the Dakota* (St. Paul, MN: Minnesota Historical Society, 2012), 173.

36 Wilson, “Carrolynn.”

38 Wilson.

38–39 Wilson.

39 Diane Wilson, interview with Carrie Cavender Schommer, Upper Sioux Community, at home, July 23, 2024.

40 Stephen Return Riggs, *A Dakota-English Dictionary* (St. Paul, MN: Minnesota Historical Society, 1992), viii.

42 *Dakota Iapi Teunhindapi* (Dakota Wicohan, 2013), 11.

44 Wilson, interview.

44 “There Were About Five of Us.”

45 “There Were About Five of Us.”

45 Carrie Schommer, Dakota Language Meeting, Lower Sioux Indian Community, Morton, MN, November 7, 2024.

Extend Your Learning

IDEAS FOR WRITING AND DISCUSSION

- What moment in this story do you think you will most remember? Why?
- Who do you believe was most important to this person's success? Why?
- What do you think were the hardest moments for this person? Why?
- How do you think this person was able to overcome hardship in their life?
- What were the happiest moments in the story of this person's life?
- What moment in the story reminded you of something in your own life?
- Write your own short autobiography, the story of your life so far!

IDEAS FOR VISUAL PROJECTS

- Draw images for three or four moments that are not illustrated in this book.
- Draw a sketch of this person and include items they liked.
- Find images from American Indian Boarding Schools from the time this book covers.
- Find historic images to share of activities this book mentions. Are they different now?
- Find historic images to share of the reservations or places this book mentions.

- Make a map of tribal nations near where you live. Where are reservations located? What tribes live there? What else did you learn about these tribal nations?

- Create a bar graph, pie chart, or other infographic on one of these topics:

    1. How many Native Americans live in urban areas near you? Which US cities are home to the largest populations of Native Americans?
    2. How many Native American students are there in your school district? How many tribes are represented?
    3. Explore "Why Treaties Matter" and give a brief report about how treaties formed the reservations and the homelands of Dakota and Ojibwe peoples.

Resources for Visual Projects

American Indian Education: Teaching and Learning
https://education.mn.gov/MDE/dse/indian/teach/

Why Treaties Matter
https://treatiesmatter.org/exhibit/

IDEAS FOR FURTHER LEARNING

The Dakota and Ojibwe people continue to live in Minnesota and are part of all aspects of our society. While English is a shared language, many Dakota and Ojibwe people also study and speak Dakota and Anishinaabemowin, their Indigenous languages.

- Find unfamiliar words in this book and create a glossary or word list with definitions.

- Create a timeline for this person's life.

- Learn how to count to ten in Dakota or Ojibwe.
- Look up Ojibwe or Dakota words for baseball or ball games such as lacrosse.
- Learn about Dakota and Ojibwe sports and activities such as powwows.
- Make a list of four common traditions the Ojibwe and Dakota share.

Resources to Learn More

Historic Fort Snelling: Educator Resources
https://www.mnhs.org/fortsnelling/learn/educator-resources

Minnesota Historical Society: Beginning Dakota
http://beginningdakota.org

Minnesota Historical Society: Minnesota Territory
http://www.mnhs.org/talesoftheterritory

Minnesota Historical Society: Ojibwe Material Culture
http://www.mnhs.org/ojibwematerialculture

The Ojibwe People's Dictionary
https://ojibwe.lib.umn.edu

About the Author

Diane Wilson is a Dakota author, educator, and bog steward. Her novel, *The Seed Keeper* (2021), and her memoir, *Spirit Car: Journey to a Dakota Past* (2006), won the Minnesota Book Awards in 2022 and 2007, respectively. She has also published a nonfiction book, *Beloved Child*, and coauthored a picture book—*Where We Come From*. Her essays have appeared in anthologies including *Kinship: Belonging in a World of Relations* (2021), *We Are Meant to Rise* (2021), and *A Good Time for the Truth* (2016). She is the former executive director for Dream of Wild Health and the Native American Food Sovereignty Alliance. In addition to this book, she authored other books in this series. Wilson is a Mdewakanton descendant, enrolled on the Rosebud Reservation.

About the Illustrator

Cole Redhorse Taylor is a Mdewakanton Dakota, enrolled with the Prairie Island Indian Community. He lives and works on his reservation community located within the traditional boundaries of Dakota homelands in Minnesota. He is a multidisciplinary artist with a BFA in fine arts studio with an emphasis in drawing and painting from the Minneapolis College of Art and Design. His works include traditional forms of drawing, painting, beadwork, quillwork, and textile work in traditional regalia. He works toward celebrating his people as thriving conduits of his ancestors' legacies and to solidify their presence. Taylor's art for this book uses the ledger art style of drawing over old documents.

About the Series Editors

Heid E. Erdrich is a member of the Ojibwe Nation enrolled at the Turtle Mountain Reservation in North Dakota. She grew up in Wahpeton, North Dakota. She is also German American and Metis from Canada. Erdrich has written several books of poetry and a cookbook focused on Indigenous foods. Along with being Anishinaabe/Ojibwe, Erdrich's extended family includes Dakota, Hidatsa, Somali American, German American, and immigrants from India. She loves the stories of how many kinds of people came to call one place home. Erdrich has lived in Minnesota for many years, raising her kids in Minneapolis, where they went to public schools.

Gwen N. Westerman is Dakota from the Sisseton Wahpeton Oyate and a citizen of the Cherokee Nation of Oklahoma. She grew up in Kansas among many different tribal nations. Today, she writes about Dakota history, and writes poetry in English and Dakota. Westerman's ancestors were teachers, leaders, and hard workers who were Dakota, Cherokee, Ojibwe, and Odawa along with a few French and Scottish traders. She lives in Minnesota, where her kids grew up playing ice hockey and soccer.